OPENERS

NINA NYHART

TEMPER

MARGO LOCKWOOD

OPENERS
Copyright © 1979 by Nina Nyhart

TEMPER
Copyright © 1979 by Margo Lockwood

All rights reserved
Library of Congress Catalogue Card Number 78-74232
ISBN 0-914086-26-X
Printed in The United States of America

Typeset by Jeffrey Schwartz at *Sojourner*

The publication of this book was supported by a grant from
the Massachusetts Council for the Arts and Humanities.

ALICE JAMES BOOKS
138 Mt. Auburn Street
Cambridge, MA 02138

OPENERS

poems by

Nina Nyhart

I would like to thank the editors of the following publications in which some of these poems first appeared: *The Andover Review, Arion's Dolphin, The Blacksmith Anthology, Dark Horse, Green House, The Little Magazine, The Nantucket Review, The Ohio Review, Poetry Northwest, The Virginia Quarterly Review, Zeugma.*

My gratitude to The MacDowell Colony where many of these poems were written.

CONTENTS

RABBITS vs. WIND

Later we'll be found:
carcasses in brambles, sunlight piercing the septums.
In the real woods, density
won't save us.

Inventing ourselves—
not lazing while the tortoise tankwalks by
or blundering into a spaniel's jaws
or breeding ourselves silly in cages,
crazed for wild carrots—we become

who we'll die for:
pulse, fur, ears thin as leaves.
When I face the wind I remember this,
smelling the loss to come,
prepared to play.

SOMEBODY NAMED McGRATH

Somebody named McGrath is keeping track of my life.
He doesn't write or phone or stand over my unmade
bed. He doesn't appear when I'm dreaming my old
dreams.

McGrath, bless you, come closer, and he doesn't.

McGrath, cut through the garbage in this alley and
shine on me, he doesn't.

Alright, McGrath, hear this, I'm coming after you,
and I hurtle through thin air, collapse exhausted
on a floor of spilt rage.

But there are days when I'm happy, when I can almost
hear someone laughing. There's no one behind me.
I'm alone and happy still. I think McGrath is
taking notes.

When I weep for no reason except I'm alive with
sadness, McGrath remembers everything I'm trying
to forget.

THANK YOU

You stood on my bed, sheet over
your head, arms spread wide,
a huge white seaskate, triangular

and looming. Then your nightgown
flew up, I saw another triangle:
black, but your head was gray so

it was me too, and then your mother
was there and it was all of us—
grandmother/mother/ daughter
les exposeuses.

Thank you for that moment
of pure geometry, for my strange
gray hair in childhood negatives,
for each night's nightmare you planted

and forgave. Then I turned in sleep,
lost on your lawn, staring up
at the damp dogwood in full bloom.

SEEING THROUGH TREES

The trees don't think, but I want them to:
    birch to have tapered silvery thoughts,
    spruce—a prickly mind, hemlock—dark
    metaphysics.

Let pear examine passion and elm brood on
    destiny. Someone has to consider important
    matters.

If you know trees are people, why not admit
    it.

                    Oak

                    You carve a heart
                    in me
                    grayskin, grandfather

        Apple

        No neat red dots
        on a green circle
        but arthritic, sprawled

        I climb you
        to prove something
        shake you for fun

        fall straight down
        like an apple

Weeping Willow

But you don't, do you
unsad tree, up to your neck
in unsaid plans

Roots race like spies
sniff out any drop, hunt springs
tie knots in water pipes

I wouldn't trust a tree like that
keeping a fiend's grasp underground
pretending long green tears

Mountain Ash

You want to fly
They say it's impossible

You want to live forever
They say you'll die

So you arch your green feathers
and burst and burst

into flame-berries

Maple

I'm trying to learn
your language:

color turns, dropped leaves
I can't translate
may never

Still, I strain
for that first infinitive

to change

OTHER SNOW

No, it's not the same snow. You wish it were that other snow falling on you soft as a nightgown, and you walked out warm in the white night, pressing your cheek to treebark, hoping to become a tree yourself.

Then you wouldn't have to say goodbye to a living soul.

THE STRING OF MY ANCESTORS

When I need string I can't find it,
but today
string is everywhere.

Shame on the one who
does not want string.

I must not forget my ancestors.
I do up packages:
little gold cars and ivory servants
for their new lives.

I must not forget my children.
I teach them cats' cradles:
Jacob's Ladder, The Bridge and The River,
to keep them out of mischief.

I tie bows on my children's fingers.
They must not forget
their ancestors.

When you cut string
it crawls off
in two directions.

GREEN BULLDOGS

Families like that never split up, grouped around a piece of white shelf, a homefire burning. You stroke them, rearrange them, know who's mama and papa, who's little.

You know how the real ones get born, the sticky pushing, you love them, don't touch. But these cool china ones, feel that smooth haunch. If you can love a green ceramic bulldog, who can say who's coming next.

VOCATION

I wanted to be a surgeon but
when I put a scalpel near someone's heart
it might come out between the back ribs
for instance because I have faulty
depth perception they said   how did I feel
about Public Health   Okay I said picturing
the gray building not wanting to hurt them
They tested me for manual dexterity and
ideophoria   said I'd make a terrific

window decorator   I went home decorated
my window with little white paper cutout
stars and moons on the black panes   Looks
really nice my mother said   They asked me
to write on what would happen if the sun
didn't shine and I wrote more words than
anyone ever   they said that's a record
I said what's it good for   they said
we don't know but you're young yet

A TALL GIRL

You can't hear me can you so I'll
say it   you're so tiny tiny   you are
toy people toy cars toy brains   I
thought when I was growing up and
up we live in a nation of dwarves
no wonder there's trouble   your
gardens will overtake you   wrap
their tendrils around your tiny
ears your little necks   my legs
stuck out between crib bars   they
shoved them back   my hips ached
growing pains they said   damn right
with fingers like that you can only
shake hands with yourself   stop
whispering they said   I said I'm
shouting but the wind is blowing
the words away   they handed up bricks
to put on my head   taught me to smoke
I'm puffing away on my herringbone patio
I want a lover I said   they said what
we can't hear you   what's that

HAYDN'S CADILLAC

White, what else, and inside:
trapeze artists chicken farmers shoe
merchants   parked at a camp by the sea
in Nebraska   that's how it FELT I was
taking lessons in chromatic art and
chromosome manipulation   a well balanced
program   no room for argument
so I agreed to what you said in the back
seat   committed myself to music
for life and all that goes with it

Haydn, honey, I'm still in here but
your staying would've changed everything
we'd drive south learn spirituals
eat prawns go sailing have kids
mow the lawn   why'd you say
"Liebchen, you nefer listen!"
iron pipe rapping my knuckles
your mouth a dusty old prairie
galloping toward me I must have
learned SOMETHING didn't I didn't I

HALLELUJAH

You give me the world as it is: terrific.
But I never asked, we never agreed. Begging
the issue, I hoist my thumb for a lift
elsewhere: Route 3, the ferry, Nantucket.
And you've come, too, lugging your pail
of facts, ready to sift them before me,
or fling them in my face.

　　　　　　　This time I'll grab one,
dunk it in relaxing fluid, press and frame
it for you and you'll be so joyful you'll
leap to embrace me, knock over the bucket
releasing the rest which fall into the sea.

We're uncommonly light.
Dock, island, coast, globe dwindle—
we dance on the tiny blue head of a pin.

THE SHIRT

with the button
that hangs by a thread
the one you wear sailing,
the one with the knife
in the pocket, the initials partly unstitched,

lies in my lap. I'm stitching
the blue initials back on. The shirt
was a present from me. The knife
lies in the pocket and the button
dangles. We're barely sailing,
searching for threads

of wind. I'm trimming the threadbare
collar and stitching
and watching the sail
and fingering the shirt.
Then I unbutton
the pocket that holds the knife.

Keeping the knife
tightly in hand I rethread
the needle with white and sew on the button.
The elbows are frayed, the old stitches
undone, but the shirt
is your favorite. I glance at the sail

and your back and my hand. Suddenly the sail
snaps out like a knife
and the water splits open—the shirt
rises up and the blue and white threads
and the jagged stitches
brush over my face. The buttons,

the elegant buttons,
like little pearl boats, sail
down my cheek stitching
a path, and the knife
falls into the water. The wind dies, the thread
lies tangled. I fold up the shirt,

rebutton the knifepocket.
We are sailors again, threading
home—new stitches, a ragged shirt.

A CURIOUS PROBLEM

You're on the other side of the river.
Here: 5 cannibals, 3 canoes, a fox and
a goose. I'm the missionary with the backpack
full of grain. Monkeys and mangoes on both
sides. You have 2 horses and 1 ferry.
The ferryman, on my side, says it's Tuesday,
and a crocodile, smiling, asks if I need
a lift.

You mount your horse and wave. I flicker
a grin back. It looks like we'll meet
midstream, and on time. I think we'll make
some exchange there in the rushing water,
then clamber up opposite banks, pause
for a second—kind to our animals—then note
we're the same distance apart as before.

We are dauntless.

Two trains will be leaving soon.

ANNIVERSARY QUILT

Wills	crisp	denim	beard	warms
Annes	cheek	Fifty	years	Their
apron	cabin	green	field	child
years	After	barns	dance	after
fires	after	songs	Under	linen
under	wools	under	plaid	rings
lilac	polka	Night	frays	edges
Spoon	hours	Blood	slyly	laces
ferns	Strip	groom	shirt	fling
bride	dress	leave	seams	Silks
curve	twine	enter	sewed	hills
Birds	trees	fruit	burst	Crazy
roses	track	geese	Petal	thorn
vines	marry	sleep	Ohios	skies
spill	stars	moons	Fifty	woven
Wills	patch	Annes	faded	heart

THE CHILDREN

Kissing wrinkles is what they hate.
They're scared of contagion, of waking one morning
    with lines in their own foreheads.
They don't want to growl or drool or say ''dear.''
They want to keep their open eyes and their pink hands.
They want to touch the sprouts in the garden and learn
    to pat the dragon.
They will not grow old and they stamp their feet
    and make faces.
Each stamp pushes them a little taller.
Their faces make their faces.

THE BLANKET

Each summer I unpack the World War I army blankets and take one to my cabin where I try not to write about it: an ode in praise of its many outstanding qualities: durability, warmth, indifference to the bodies it has covered. This one, the color of camouflage, has no ears, yet it extracts promises from me concerning honor and history and harsh beauty, and though I fight the urge to make too much of it, the blanket rises and assumes the form of my grandfather, swaying above my paper.

THE POSITION

I want to attain the correct distance from everything and everyone including those I love, including the trees and rocks I bump into, including the dog who likes to be petted and the wild animals who avoid me as I walk through the woods, including the ideas batting through darkness which move me in peculiar ways so that I must research the correct position once again.

THE TYPEWRITER

There's not a lot of poetry in this. What
    can you do with a metal typewriter.
    Everything I say turns hard and black.

By day it's a machine. At night it becomes
    the machine of its dreams: harder, blacker.

Funny lines, sad lines, it's all the same
    to the typewriter. A person could die of
    a wrenching passion and the keys would
    maintain their perfect equilibrium.

My fingers don't want to meet so many of the dead;
    fingers live in a country where each day
    new cells spring to life without being asked.

Now I ask you, who would put this kind of thing
    between us, a hard box that stamps out
    what I mean to sing.

SCARECROW CONSIDERS ORIGINS

Questions:
    Am I made?
    Am I a speechless immigrant—feet in soil,
        head in sky—or nightmare roost,
        blind observer, guardian of vegetables?

Answers:
    Yes.
    Immigrants speak among themselves, a head
        in the sky is worth two in the bush,
        friends perch, the blind listen,
        vegetables depend.

Then call me King Furrow,
    beacon for birds,
        defender of the law of rows
        and register of winds
            as long as straw will last.

SCARECROW'S DREAM

I think it's June—
crows landing in black waves.

Farmer arrives with his 22.
Stop, I say. And put away

that gun, I'll handle this.
Farmer shrugs, strides off.

For once I'm boss, and we're
a circle of friends. We discuss,

make deals: a little corn—
a little reticence. Come at night—

save your life. Peaceable
kingdom I'm thinking when

I feel a step on my shoulder,
the first peck in my eye.

SCARECROW ON DESTINY

mole race finishes
underground
rabbit
   curls around her death

pumpkins rot
berries melt
maggots gulp
   the meat of squirrel

my shadow thins
   i too will be dinner

   and earth richer
washed down in green
in red   in brown
   in time   *in time*

SCARECROW'S SONG WHEN FARMER PLOWS

carves grass down to loam
to worms down to blood

curves into furrow
cleaves root-throb and cell

lifts globe and marrow
drives deeper through earth

through blue-dusted corpus
bursts plasma and cosm

blasts atom past time
white ocean   blood light

on a glistening blade
his own field opens

SCARECROW PERMITTING

Scarecrow says:

> Farmer, may I
> take a step?

No answer:
no farmer:
no step

Scarecrow says:

> *why did you*
> *hold me down*
> *extract*
> *essentials*
> *transfuse fear*
> *name me*
> *leave me*
> *extremities*

Scarecrow says:

> Why "may I?"

Scarecrow says:

> I may
>   I will
>   I am walking

SQUARES: PORTRAIT OF A CARPENTER

Meal

He likes it plain: meat, potato,
greenery, pie. Each evening,
swallowing what grows above ground
and below: cow's moo, stretch of roots,
fruit's glow, he pats his belly, rubs
the smooth table, loving his hand-
made furniture, grain of the tree,
the miracles in his stomach.

Peg

His love, a sturdy miss. She minds
her manners, seems, in the village
to be like the others. But her
apron won't billow, she's knees and
elbows, flickering lashes, rough
perimeters. Two stiff braids march
down her school-straight back. He's edgy.
Nothing suggests a future fit.

Wheel

His invention: the one with four
sides. Bold! Revolutionary!
Surely a cart on four of these
won't roll off the globe. Still, you can't
be sure. Best to tie it down, fence
it in, buy a dog with vicious
parents. Then he can rest, saw wood
prone, dream up another advance.

One

Beginning again, the ex-King
of Right Angles discovers new
shapes: bowed horizon, crescent moon,
the arc of Peg's smile. He could top
the Taj, build her a flying glass
pagoda. Or do what he knows—
lay out the old, the infinite
room: one mind long by one mind wide.

PAINTING

I'm painting the floor of my room. I'm sure it's the largest roo
m I've ever seen. I'm painting it blue to match my lungs, in str
ips from one wall to the other. It must be about two acres or so
but it's still pretty early. I'm not tired even though I've done se
veral strips already. I'm doing it backwards, painting until my
back hits the wall, then I turn and paint where I was just standi
ng. Then I start back in the other direction. Mmmmmm. All t
his blue. It must be midday now although I don't have a watc
h. You don't really need a watch when you're doing something
this interesting, painting blue paint on this two acre floor. I'm
thinking about flying. I can almost see clouds in this floor. Rea
dy for the last strip. I slow down to really enjoy this last one, br
eathe in the lovely paint smell, like real sky. You're wonderin
g how I'm going to get out of here. Don't worry, when I get to
the corner I'm going to take a deep breath, and think about wi
ngs.

THE BABY

It is gone entirely. The people think it will never happen again. But it does, over and over. No matter what poundage the baby, no matter what kind the water. People think: if we try harder to remember it will not happen again. They tie colored strings to their fingers, strings on the baby's toes and fingers. The bath becomes a rainbow of loops and ties: vermilion puce artichoke persimmon lime magenta. And then seeing those strung colors the baby laughs with delight. The people think: the baby is laughing. But why? And then while the baby is still laughing and the people are still wondering why they all get on one side of the tub, tip it up and give the laughing baby the heave ho. Then they look down at their hands and say: Uh oh.

BRIEF LECTURE SERIES

A Brief Lecture On Reason

There's a reason for everything. The reason for the St. Petersburg-Tampa airport is that there were no hyphenated names in Florida. Now, after the operation, large numbers of people arrive and depart. More travel and the spread of compromise.

Considering the many presently detached cities of this world, we may conclude that the linkage rate will swiftly ascend as reason extends its tentacles, through airports, into the future.

A Brief Lecture On Conscience

It's here to stay. Here. And here. You can almost enjoy the ubiquity of it while at the same time not know exactly where it'll gnaw its way in. Sits there barking until you give it a bone, then happily licks your leg.

I ask myself whether these germs are contagious, and what about vivisection and other carnal questions, but myself is yapping about a missing leg.

A Brief Lecture On Big Words

Lately you've been using words like "floccipaucinihilipili-fications" and I advise you against it. Big words tend to numb the senses, and one might question *any* word that contains no e's meaning "the act of estimating things as being worthless."

In future, I recommend sticking with small words—ones that slip easily off the tongue and tiptoe into the ear like a stream of ants carrying thought-jars on their heads.

THE SENTENCES

The lock's sentence is to keep swallowing strangers and
  the key's sentence is never to be recognized.

The sentence of the door is not to remember its two names.

The wall's sentence is to march without stopping and the
  sentence of the ceiling is to watch its brother the floor.

The sentence of the chair is never to close its arms.

The table's sentence is to lie still under the knives of tears.

The sentence of paper is to be loved by insects and the pen's
  sentence is to listen to its own long scratches.

The sentence of words is to be eaten slowly, the final meal.

DREAM CHILD

I gave birth to this remarkable baby talking at such an early age in three part perfectly constructed sentences. Now baby is speaking in paragraphs with indentations, in theses novels tomes paperback editions.

Oh remarkable baby how is it you know so much how is it your life and lingo are so vast how do you talk faster and better and more than any of us. Why are you growing why are you gray why are you dying taking your stream of words with you. And why am I waking just as I went to sleep—alone and empty.

THE FIRST DAY OF YOUR PENCIL

The first day of your pencil should be delicately handled—bring irises and lilies. They'll bloom around the pencil reminding it of its origin the forest and its future: a story called "Death Of A Pencil."

Curious pencil does its work, enters the future line by line, comes close, closer to the end of the story. How can a pencil avoid it, shoved across the page, scribbled headlong into a flat-topped, ground-down stub.

THE WINDOW

Everyone knows the window is cracked, mullions and frame peeling, its thin gray curtains brushing the old sill. Anyway, you stand there looking out.

Men and women dressed in black and white turn with the road like a story. You watch them going down to the river, dust on the road, dogs barking, lovers carrying baskets. Your eyes are on fire, starving. They wave back to you, calling, you think. The day shines through you onto the floor.

Sometimes you feel you are on the road looking up at the window. You in the empty road and the window upstairs at the corner of the house. Suddenly the sun turns the window to flames. Then you remember you are still in the room, looking out.

A breeze lifts the curtains. The people are coming back now, long shadows stretch out before them. They almost trample their own shadows. You close the window. Darkness enters, settling like smoke around your glass feet.

S IS FOR SUCCESS

There was a man who loved his wife more than anything in this world. He loved her eyes and her hair and her ears her tongue her arms her breasts her belly her sex hips thighs he loved her so much he said darling I want to keep you forever I want to hold you wrap myself around you eat you up. Which he did.

He was a hard worker. He worked so hard cleaning sewers he got the job of hauling stones and he worked so hard at that he got to take the corpses to their graves and he did that so well he was promoted to scrubbing the shadows off the fields and he did that so well he got the job of stringing stars.

So he sits up there stringing stars with the woman in his belly wondering what his next step should be.

LOVE'S HIGH HOOPS

Love, with your high hoops, keep running
and here's a stick.

Love, take these stilts, it's hard to see
you in the tall grass.

Love, here's one more orange to juggle.

Love, with your noon blaze and promise,
your smile, why am I still talking to you when
you've fallen off your stilts, dropped oranges,
let hoops roll away and you lie there in the
meadow laughing at me. I only asked you to turn
one more somersault,

Now get out of here, clown. Who could trust
anyone so inept.

THE PAST

It's your turn. Dig a hole, put it in, dirt on top, smooth it over. Mushrooms may spring there, or wildflowers. In either case we'll have done something good, as good as the woods. Trees fall, decay, build the forest floor, and the others tree on. We're going on too, without this heavy load.

TACKLING THE FUTURE

It falls easy as thunder, clunking against the ground.

Oh Future, Get up! Here's a hand, the one that's always after you, after you.

Oh, Future, you're so pristine, we hate to spoil—still, you're rather nice with grass stains on your bottom—imprints of tiny damaged blades, and that stunned look.

Now let's give you another hand, not for what you can do for us, but simply for being on the field each day when we walk out.

ARCHAEOPTERYX

Maybe you didn't know what you wanted to do and that's
    why you had bird feathers but teeth in your beak
    and claws on your wings. Some days I, too, have the
    wishbone of a bird and a reptile's brain.

I like your name better than archipelago or asterisk,
    and I want to meet you here by the reservoir where
    the suburban Labradors have lost their natural enmity
    for mallards, where we also have trouble remembering
    what we're supposed to do besides step up our heartbeats
    and clear our lungs.

As I walk round and round I imagine you sweeping in—
    hellbent on feeding or nesting, carrying in your beak
    a complex, reassuring message.

Archaeopteryx, I hold out my hand across one hundred and
    ninety million years for you to light on.

TEMPER

poems

MARGO LOCKWOOD

George Lockwood

Acknowledgments are due the following publications in which some of these poems appeared: *Blacksmith Anthology—Volume 2, Green House, Hanging Loose, The Massachusetts Review, Nantucket Review, The Painted Bride, Ploughshares, Pool* (University of Massachusetts), and from the volume, *Three Poems Written in Ireland,* Menhaden Press, 1977.

CONTENTS

YOUNG DANCER

I used to dance for my grandmother,
a ritual dance, when she would drink
too much, and I would promenade
and waltz in old lace gowns.

I would often end my pirouettes
wrapped in her ecru nylon curtains
tight against the wall.
It was a ball.

Dressed in her night gowns
I would soar, from couch to chair arm
surefooted as Pavlova,
and she would wave me on,
the tinkle of ice in her old-fashioned glass
all the audience noise I needed.

She died three years later,
but every so often when no one is around,
I take a double of whatever's there
and go leaping through my house,
laughing uproariously
for no good reason.

A card shark to her family and her set,
I was her first granddaughter,
born after a long night of in-law poker.

Now in my late thirties, I hope
I am coming into her scornful eye,
the set of certainty in the mouth,
the easy reliance on something shadowy
and far back and Prussian,
that is iron in the spine

that let her displace her griefs
as if they were elements of the game.

3:15

For my pantheism
to become religion
all it takes is a certain time of day

the light through trees
linden trees shattering the light
at the edge of water
near some New England lake

all I know is that they are
greenish aluminum on the undersides,
linden, alder, aspen—

and they clatter in the wind
in a way that made me learn their names

BLIZZARD

The sound the blizzard made
when stopped
was like a plug for both ears,
unlike Zen
most like New England under glass

or under fathoms of white
frozen dreams

dreams the summer had
when June was thickening
the breath past pleasure.

DECEMBER ECLIPSE

The birds
confused by the angle
of light during the eclipse
resumed their getting up,
squawking & complaints.

I stood on the beige-grained sidewalk
in my town facing east
and positioned the hardware store's
gingerbread roof between me
and the sun's angle.

Within fifteen minutes
saw the rick-rack become a scalloped jumble
of not exact shadow,
of vague definitions.

The geese or gulls
that headed south all month
along the Beacon Street car-tracks
started to veer and wonder
what was up, their v's wavering

and the sky took on
a veil of gray
with the weaker sun
still flickering
and making motes sunlike,

casting ambiguous shadows
of telephone poles and parking meters
thickened and grayed
on the ground
like totems of fading skywriting.

I hoped like eskimos or hawaiians
my townspeople would run amok

come pouring out of bank and bar
to orgiate on the corner
of Washington & Beacon,

but they must have learnt
in school to stay indoors
when the sun is acting up,
and not look up like Lot's wife
looking back, or smoke a piece of glass
& participate in the cosmos
like a peeping tom.

AGAIN, SPRING

When I notice red pin-head spores
hemstitching the moss
of the swampy bank

I admit I am dragging my feet
entering this season again.

White sale of the ragged crocus,
self-advertisement of the quince,
cerise & florid with its rheumy center—
all the mindless greenness setting forth,

takes time for me to summon my response
due to disheartening weather in the world.

Hope is still fragile
as a wax flower in a burning house.

But a cardinal in my backyard
flames as if to crack my window
with his red;

and myths untuck their skirts
in this inhuman, unconscionable spring.

ANONYMOUS

I did time with marriage.
Time when my beauty,
if it was, I think
was youth, and it
bloomed and in pregnancy upon pregnancy
twice and twice over
grew flaccid
and my face paled
and my eyes for years
were gray or faded blue.

Now I pick up men as I browse through bookstores,
aware, as I finger their spines thoughtfully,
men's, books',
that there could be some ideas & energies
too swift & dark
for my handling.

With men & ideas
that's half the charm:
only certain kinds of men
understand me or my ideas,
and that's my charm
if it's that
and not just wildness
or swiftness or darkness.

ANALYSIS AND A BLUE & WHITE JUG

A candle burns beside the bed.
Someone in midwinter
has put white daisies
in a blue & white jug.

Wind stirs the white curtains.
They furl voluptuously
in the dawn.

This is what you notice
when you are about to crack in two
from desire.
You need that cool eye.

DAMNED CALENDAR

I tore off the beautiful month
of October.
It was a nothing month
filled with things to do,
so I filled up the days
with dentists, movies, musicales,
classes.

Leaves fell,
as they do then.
Skeletons of elm and oak and maple
appeared suddenly.

The air snapped.
A trolleyman said ''Rosy Cheeks!''
as if he chided me;
some movingmen salute me
with their trucky horn.

I march around.
A new stripe appears
on the sleeve of my winter coat.

Not for good conduct,
for patience.

SLOTH IN THE LAND OF THE PURITAN ETHIC

Like Oblomov sitting his life out
between muslin sheets
laundered by kulaks,

here in America where everyone
who can work, works at two or three
occupations or their hobbies
obsess them beyond sense,

it is poetic to be meager and dim
about certain things
when everything is surging the other way.

Conservation
is a deliberate act of the will,
not the saving of flattened and greasy
tin cans for suburban virtue.

There is no guilt
to notice the incidents
one needs to,

how dust scales the lilac leaves
after their hearts spread out
a month in the raw of nature.

But to make the bank manager understand,
that would tax Thoreau.

FEARS OF WOMEN

I'm not afraid of the dark,
have lain in bed hours,
watching shadows flicker
from swiss lace curtains
onto a white wall
after midnight.

Or money.
At lawyers' rooms, with bankers,
I'm as cool as a madam
in a big city house.

Or horses, or locomotives.

Death is so grand and final
it's hard to quail before it
as if it were a beast or a mugger.

And the ocean has been merely something
at the beach since childhood.

A woman won't react
to its vast maternity
with the dread of men.

Cities, beggars, blind men
sordidness, do not appall.

Just high diving,
and I'm frightened to death
of love, the only time
I'm strange.

A BOY

His arms are thin in the lamplight
on the long table. Floods of yellow
and amber light holding the June roses

in suspension with him, his tan
touched with a few scabs of baseball.

A bead of blood has loosened itself
from his wrist and glints like a ladybug
as he turns it in the light,
the spectator at his blood like a boy
scientist, watching a world
in microscope view.

Writing this poem about him
is like hurling myself in front of
the moving truck of the world, stopped
fractionally before my eyes,
like his all-of-a-sudden externalized life.

DAUGHTERS

Now the young women
that they are
go moving through my house
and they grow strange to me.

The brown haired girls
I still see kodachromed
in matching smocks
in a springlike haze
with bloodroot flowers
dying in their hands
shimmer in my focus
like something seen under water.

Their fat baby faces have grown bones
and have planes & a spirited color
that make men look at them
as we walk through our town.

SCHOOL PICTURES

My boy is the one
in the picture
sticking out his tongue
his eyes crossed.

Believe me, I am relieved
the children are turning out
a little silly, like I did.

I was concerned
that the heavy weight of things
might somehow start to press on them

that seeing me cry or get drunk
now and then would swerve them
away from the way I like to live,

that their little friends
who size us up by the condition
of our lives, the strange anachronisms
of furniture and relatives we sport
abundantly,

would slant them all wrong,
that they would start to apologize,
turn toady, wrinkle up—

instead of upholding
our fine family traditions
of gooniness, eccentricity and revenge.

VICTORIAN GRANDMOTHER

In the pinch of time, facing
an upright piano under its
paisley throw

you sport a jet and agate necklace
around your freckled throat.

You were mad for costume jewelry—
and better if it was red,
and soon you ran off
to marry Handsome Jack.

I strain my ears after
your songs, you had a gift
for whistling
with a wild vibrato like a finch;

& people liked to say
while working on potato salad
in the kitchen that old one
about whistling girls & cackling hens—
you showed them.

Whatever else I inherited
I wear a brooch of yours,
a bright wing of a butterfly

fixed under a glass bead—
it's caught there, iridescent & rusty
strung on a knotty silver chain

it carries your memory effortless—
like a sure thing.

THE DARK GIRL, THE LIGHT GIRL

Summer was at a midpoint, and the blackberries
underfoot had little of red about them,
so far had the ripening taken.

When two sisters grew together,
but grew into trouble.

One was disorganized by illness
of the mood, to the point where
hospitals were sanctuary

The other was like Martha to her sister,
bearing her up like a caryatid
through months of withdrawal & emptiness

until the spiralling of nonsense
caught the first girl up
and she is lost to us

by her own hand, if something so unsatisfactory,
damning & despair-filled can be said
to be handiwork.

She is well out of it,
for the extent of chaos
and the will to endure it

is always being measured to fit us
like a suit of clothes; bright or dark,
which we wear as long as we can,
like the other orders of creation,

until we age and grow silent
as this girl did in what time we think
is premature,

but may have been fitted to her
by unconscious mercies
acting in concert around her.

In memoriam, Victoria Nyhan, 21, Cape Elizabeth, Maine

A YOUNG MAN'S SMELL

In the foyer of my borrowed house
saying goodbye to young men

what is so mortal
as this smell of a young man?
He has a beard; they all have beards,
sometimes black, sometimes curly and blond.

In his fresh laundered shirt
arm over your shoulder
he wishes you goodbye
a good trip
his smell is young
like an animal
or a son.

His hand a spear in your side
his smile the moon
torn from the flesh of the earth

Who am I
to worry about the death of young men?
their pleasant company, faint scent
of their skin through the cotton
of their summer shirts?

It is my fault
memory causes this stitch in my side
making me into a kohl-eyed ravaged
virago, like Anais Nin, like Marina
Tsetsaeva, guttering faithfully
for all the young men
till they put themselves out.

EROTIC LENTEN ALLOWANCE

I have allowed myself
to speak of you briefly.

I ride home from the quiet red-lit
bar where I savored anecdotes
in which you figured,
as a dragon
figures in a tapestry.

The Charles River was a platter of black sinuosity, the lights
stood up on stilts in its shine.

I woke up to myself
out of the fiction of my everydays
and in the radio's tin music,

the sand which coats the gutters
spreading dirt over snow
until white is black
and the air is grey or pewter
from the fallout of fighting winter,

I sang like a madwoman,
I was replete with memories
like a china cabinet filled with favorites,

through which I shuffled
like a gambler who cannot lose.

MOTEL MAN

I should have known,
flying like a dizzy, overladen moth
to visit this candidate for my body
and its weekend rise in temperature

when we took a post-coital swim
at four in the afternoon
and the cross-country trucks
roared by outside the chain-link fence.

And we even smoked, leaving our filter-tips
hanging over the concrete abutment
of our grottoed pool, bobbing with salesmen
in the chlorinated blue.

Should have known it would come to naught
but a memory squashed like a bug
under my thirty-three year old thigh
erupting like a blister of languor,
but easy by now to forget.

CELEBRATION IN JULY

We both agreed it was hot.
I wondered about passion
but sweated. My discomfort
was precise.

You scalded me
with your thighs, and
I burnt you,
I suppose,
with my comparative youth.

Ovens of love
that burn everything up
I am ashen from places
where I can't return.

But I digress. It was sweet,
a monoprint of marriage, a week-end
dalliance, a half-hearted
could-have-been-something
time.

Enough pain and knives
of reality
to make me refuse
every other such intimacy.

Like the coming together
of primitives,
it was sufficient to change me.

REMINDER

Arms around me, tongue in my mouth
he was just a cliché
I couldn't listen to again.

Beard, a tired rose in his buttonhole,
a tweed jacket & a few jokes at the door.

Watching his sex come up
was as distant a thing
as viewing oil rigs on TV
at work in the North Sea.

Why, when I hadn't thought of you in years,
why after faint arousal
did I spend the whole next day
composing letters, gnashing my hands,
laughing uncannily, figuring out
the odds, the angles & the handicaps

sending my letters off
like an air marshall winging
stunt pilots into the kamikaze nests

of love
why? when I even think
I hate the word?

It's come to that.

BARE ELEGY

I turned away
like a leaf yellowing
in a hothouse from too much
nutrient—your way of love.

I made you stand a distance
apart—cells of my kingdom
resisting your encroachment.

I didn't care.
I was a tomboy wife.
I stole your shirts, men friends
took photographs and sketched me
when you went to work.

Pregnant in a summer field,
old skirt, too much hair, stomach
out to somewhere with a baby.

I was secure in a fine blanket
of self assurance, or the light
cotton of my ignorance

like a southern girl from a poor
but proud family. Before the teeth
go, while the skin on the face is
fine, gleaming and sunburnt.

I would change those postures now,
arrange my album differently
if I could. Your book is closed.

It withered the yellowing love
in shutting. My hair turned white
within the year. I wouldn't talk
to people who said I had a lost look
about me. That was nothing new.

You stopped crowding me;
so I love your memory better—
having sifted through to the hard-core,
hard-scrabble rock, rock-bottom facts.

TEMPER

There were days when I'd burn my poems
years and years of poems
with no copies kept.

Or cut the hair that grew three years
until the day,
when all the scissors out,
my rage erupted in a vicy snare.

Or ripped my Indian embroidered blouse,
organdy and painstakingly worked,
a love offering from you
after years of working late
or too much.

This angry woman's way
I've learned by rote.
Going back in time
it's Napoleonic, Alexandrine,
it rips a country of repose to shreds,
a woman's way of making war

men back away
children move to the corners.

And yet is minimal.
Having a range only as wide
as a family stretches.

A friend once named it, wryly,
speaking of his mother,
kitchen grief.

ONE WAY

A strange month.

I buy fifteen yards
of what you called "oldlady chintz"

with triumphant partridges
within toile scrollery
eating pale orange and yellow pears
in a chippendale print
whose opulence
reminds me of our life

some years ago,
to be exact
as I often now
am not.

I catch myself pulling shreds
of lavishness around me
for associations of comfort
they still summon.

Each month I fall further
to the bottom of the middle class.

And though I am secure
with my monthly social welfare check

I am tempted to buy, cold cash
a green Porsche coupe
and drive it off the Mystic River Bridge
to you

sealed in a coffin of that lacquer green
we liked so much.

ROAD MAP

New willows slantwise in the sun
blow all their chartreuse stripes
in diagonal flags.

Spring in a silent parade
thins my blood with surprise
that it still causes me alarm
& amazement.

Vertical slips of tulips
stand in the brown mud—
the soldiery of May.

By accident
I drove to a town
near my husband's grave.

Nine years of memory
and the shoots still burn
in the pale yellow morning.

Aluminum bristle
of roadside tree bark
flies by in multiple disorder,
topped off with the red haze
of renewal.

As if I fight through underbrush
still I shiver with reluctant flesh

until the here-and-now
grows metallic again
and I am just a woman
grown tired of driving.

AUGUST FIELD

From the house, it was the spread-out
apron, a flat theatre
of loose-strife & thistle,

rimmed with pines
that caught the sun
on the tops after four o'clock.

We never should have bought the house.
It was too much: the land, the view,
the May grass we sat down upon
to compute interest, taxes
& the endless borrowing we'd
have to do.

But of course we did, & poured
our pockets out, & calloused our hands
with planers, adzes, sanders, routers;

they must have been dreaming up tools
for us to find, in the hardware store
we always went to.

The little time we had
for viewing our breathtaking meadow
was like gold ripped from a mine.
I would abashedly pick flowers for his desk.
Lobelia, marguerite daisies, lupine,
in a marmelade jar.

That was my life: that house, him,
& the babies, for three excessive years,
until he pushed himself too hard,
and the foundation he lived on, went.

OUTWARD BOUND

Driving the Maine roads
that always before seemed so benevolent
so vacationland—

the air seems charred with metal now,
as if a life sustaining chemical
or perfume has been taken out.

I see the sign she must have seen
in so much trouble, with her lungs
and heart filling up, and signals
all awry—

her invalid husband beside her
frightened to a peak of attention.

O blue hospital sign on the road!

There will never be a journey
I am on that spares me the sight of you

and with the round blue disc
with white H for Hospital
will come a small angina of my own
that remembers her

remembers the night, the name of the Maine town,
the phone booths and the voices disembodied,
who told the news that was all news
because it was all bad.

Dark hole in the night's midst,
low spot in the valley of eventfulness
that was my mother's life

from which determinedly brothers, their wives,
children, my father, all scrambled, all climbing
out and away from

as amateur mountaineers move,
pitching up through brambles and weeds
on one of those survival mountain schools
that charge tuition
whether you live or die.

PRIMER

After he died
I went to Europe
applying the continent
like a mustard plaster
to a bone ache.

Modern as perversion,
I wondered what hurt,
and where, and was this
happiness?

The tombs were what I liked,
& churches & stone walls.

They all made sense to me,
their shapes echoing inside
myself in a sober rondo.

I learnt the names of a few
wild flowers, some children's
stories in another tongue,
geography with a different locus.

It was all right, Europe,
not a broken-up collage
as others find it,
travelling from wholeness
to take it in,

more, it was just hills to me,
and towns, stones in formations
I was not familiar with, slopes
where I slept like a child or a
cowboy, freshened by the air
moving new over old things.

MONKSTOWN

I used to live
in a small Irish town
where the sea was a grey slate board
written on ceaselessly by the air.

And the wall down the hill
to the square was mealy & crumbled
as much from age as from the limits
of municipal care.

Tinkers stood round the churches
and begged, and looked in the windows
of schools, timeless because they
couldn't tell it.

And their children fought with
the school children, the town children
and my children.

Seasons surprised me all the time.
Pink cherry blossoms fell like wedding
confetti all through January
reeling down the streets so grey
and black in the wet air.

One day when I was homesick
from remembering snow and New England
rectangularity, picket fence reasonableness,
a certain straightness of opinion,
massive hills furred with trees and
not these hummocks of meek grass,
I steadied myself against the picturesque stone
work of the walls, and resolved to return,
away from gay, mad Ireland, woozy with motherland.

NAIL LETTER

In the dark, I picked up a nail
to write you a letter
on a piece of wood.

The iron point of midnight will
failed me, I couldn't send it.

I am brave like Joan of Arc
in dreams, but things shrink
back into place when I awake.

There are some tired flowers
here with me, two roses almost
turning back to black,
a flowering quince that drops
its petals everytime I move,
in an old green clay jug
that stands for Ireland.

All the lace in the windows
is like the pointillist lives
that people let one in on.

My favorites are on the north side
of the Liffey, where the windows
are just about exhausted, and the
lace is very old.

I am like a peeping tom
enjoying things that everyone
else ignores or is ashamed of,
the dirty old lace that I know
is valid, as the days gone by are.

One doesn't have to be in a museum
or happy. Sometimes the picturesque
is enough to carry you forward.

IRISH SEA

I quailed to see its greyness
in December. Long lifeboats
in Dun Laoghaire were stacked
like coffins next to the seawall.

The Lifeboat Society finds funds
easy to collect
when they recite statistics
on the seamen dying half a mile
from shore.

The sea grins like a glassy crypt
between pastel Georgian houses,
and the poor are near it too, in artisan
houses clotted near railway depots,
or straggling up from the shore.

It doesn't glitter much
being preoccupied with its rare
maritime climate

habitat for curlews & cormorants
looking less like birds
and more like rats with wings

wheeling like dark plumy rags
tossed in the gusts.

With a picnic of books
I lie on the pier, & people in bowlers
& tweed shawls pass smiling in another language.

The dreadful sky above us commutes
like a juggernaut, a Wagnerian backdrop
torn into shreds of grey chiffon

allows weather to rampage across the country
from Galway to Dublin in moments

as if Ireland were a miserly atoll
the heavens could afford to pay no heed to.

REDUCTIO AD ABSURDEM

Plain speech cannot suggest
how flat I find things
without you.

Plainsong, perhaps
its lyric moving only
within one octave.

It was an invention of monks
and now I am beginning to understand
their compression.

Like Occam's razor flaying through a theory,
my life has been reduced
to what I can get along without.

And my heart grows austere
like a Shaker's.